Project 4.9

Rosie Mayes

To Mel,

Enjoy!

Rosie x

Bonkers Hill

Published 2023 by Bonkers Hill
Copyright© 2023 Rosie Mayes

ISBN: 978-1-3999-3917-1

The moral right of Rosie Mayes to be identified as the author of this work has been asserted in accordance with the Copyright, Designs and Patents Act 1988.

rosie@ebcentre.co

Illustrations: Jane Overbury
Cover design: Design for Writers
Interior design: Daisy Editorial

Printed in the UK by JamJar Print on FSC paper

Contents

Section 1

The start of it all

Chapter 1

40961

My mother was an alien. I often wondered what it was like for her to be called that. I never asked. To look at her you would not have known. There were no tell-tale signs to suggest that she was possibly part of an advance party intent on invading Britain. It was when she spoke that her difference was most notable.

Today, she would have been called an 'immigrant'. But in the late 1930s, refugees and immigrants coming to Britain were known as 'aliens'. And if, like my mother, you were Austrian, with a distinctive German accent, you went through a process that categorised you depending on whether you were deemed to be a potential threat to the nation. My mother was a 'Category C Alien' – no threat.

After all, who would have thought that an Austrian could ever be a threat to Britain?

When my mother arrived in Britain in 1939 as a 17-year-old girl, she spoke very little English and had less than £2 to her name.

Her stay was meant to be only temporary, as she had plans and dreams of joining her recently emigrated Austrian father and building a new life together in the USA.

But the outbreak of war, being the granddaughter of a Jewish heiress, contracting tuberculosis and then being denied access to the USA on health grounds were all to reshape her life's journey.

By 1949, with no way forward to join her father in the USA and no route back to return to her Austrian motherland, Britain became my mother's permanent address.

For someone from Austria, my mother's newly adopted homeland challenged her in many ways. The English language. The English cuisine. The English etiquette. The English customs. The English currency. To name but a few.

But it provided her with some profoundly important things too – the sense of safety and belonging, the opportunity to develop a career in nursing and (something that many British people simply took for granted) the sea.

During her time at Midhurst Hospital in the 1940s, first as a tuberculosis patient and later as a nurse and ward sister, my mother befriended a fellow nurse who told fantastic tales of a magical island where she had whiled away many of her childhood holidays. My mother was captivated by her friend's stories.

For those of us who have grown up with the Radio 4 shipping forecast, and its reference to a three-and-a-half-mile-long island in the Bristol Channel, Lundy is vaguely familiar. It even featured in the opening ceremony of the 2012 London Olympic Games. Yet many who recognise its name probably would not be able to tell you exactly where it is located.

In 1950, my mother's choice of Lundy for a two-week coastal holiday destination was, like many of her life choices at that time, not a conventional one. Moreover, for an alien from a landlocked country, she did well to find it.

In 1938, it had taken my mother two days to reach Britain from Austria. In 1950, it took her nearly as long to reach her desired holiday destination.

From Midhurst, Sussex, to Ilfracombe on the coast of north Devon, she travelled 193 miles by car, train and foot. Then she boarded a small steamer and crossed 23 miles of choppy Bristol Channel waters to the sheltered shores of the 'Granite Isle' of Lundy.

And then, finally, after disembarking, she made the steep and energy-sapping climb from the tiny jettied harbour at the south of the island to the picturesque stone dwellings that nestled on its top.

Greeted with the same warmth she had experienced on her arrival to the somewhat larger island of Britain, my mother was shown to her holiday residence, settled herself into Bramble House and promptly fell in love with Lundy.

Over the next few years 'The Austrian Princess', as she was known, became a regular visitor, leasing the beloved Bramble House on a semi-permanent basis. An extroverted character by nature, she befriended many of the island dwellers and was often found in the Marisco Tavern, sitting by the log fire singing folk songs with her guitar and generally entertaining the close-knit Lundy community like their very own Maria von Trapp.

A 5'10", German-sounding, guitar-carrying woman does not exactly merge subtly with the locals who come and go off the island and it is no surprise that she received the attention and admiration of onlookers.

One such admirer was an RAF pilot who flew supplies, post and the occasional passenger to the island during his holiday.

As a trained aeronautical engineer, who would later be involved in the design of the automatic landing controls for commercial aeroplanes, as well as the vertical take-off and landing mechanism for jet fighters, simple small light aircraft provided little technical challenge to him.

Yet, on the first day that he flew my mother to the island, his plane developed an unusual, temporary yet unsolvable technical fault. And so, with nowhere to stay that night, he knocked on the door of Bramble House.

Exactly one year later, on 7th August 1954, Donald John Mayes married Eva Maria Zoref in St Helen's church on the island of Lundy.

Seven years, four weeks and three siblings after that, I was born on 4th September 1961.

Chapter 2

51.1781° N, 4.6673° W

You hear the noise of the helicopter before you see it. It appears out of the sky in a way that is reminiscent of the start of the 1970s TV series *M*A*S*H* (but without the accompanying earworm soundtrack 'Through early morning fog I see…' and 'Suicide is painless…').

Standing on Hartland Point helipad in north Devon, in March 2009, my excitement at visiting Lundy for the first time was like that of a child on a snowy Christmas morning. My visit had been prompted by a friend's recent thought-provoking question: 'Have you ever been to Lundy?' and my simple and spontaneous answer 'No'. Followed, moments later, by 'Not yet!'

I had grown up in a house where Lundy artefacts were as much part of the family script as references to Stoke City's football scores, whose turn it was to walk the dog and my Austrian grandfather's tuneful flatulence.

There were the first-day cover stamps from Lundy that my brother collected; the picture of a puffin on the wall of our holiday cottage; the RNLI Christmas card that arrived each December from the retired Lundy lighthouse keeper; and the photographs of my windswept parents on their wedding day outside St Helen's church.

When I first researched 'how to get to Lundy' I discovered that, during the winter months, the unpredictability of the weather and sea conditions meant that the only commercially timetabled transport for tourists was not by boat, as my mother had done, but by helicopter.

And so it was that my first visit to Lundy in 2009 was by air.

The choreography of the helicopter routine is delightful. It arrives mid-morning from Liskeard, Cornwall, and, with the motor running, sits restlessly on Hartland Helipad 'H' just long enough for it to be loaded with an assortment of bags, island supplies and passengers, before lifting off into the sky for its six-minute journey to Lundy.

The flight is fabulous. You take off from a Devon cliff edge, fly out over the sea and then, in no time at all, the ragged Lundy coastline comes into view. You find yourself transported towards the toylike island with its green fields, drystone walls, animals that look like tiny specs and Monopoly-sized dwellings. With skilful simplicity, the helicopter lands in a field flanked on one side by a path that leads to the tavern and island office, whilst on the other side sits St Helen's church.

My first experience of a helicopter ride had been a 40th birthday treat eight years earlier, but nothing prepared me for the bombardment of feelings and emotions I experienced in March 2009. As I stepped out of the helicopter and onto Lundy soil, with the deafening noise of the rotor blades overhead, the cold cutting through my ineffective windproof coat and the smell and taste of the sea in the air, I took one look at the building where my parents had been married 58 years before and, overcome by emotion, dissolved into floods of tears.

Like my mother before me (and many tens of thousands of other people since) I too fell in love with the Granite Isle and it was to play a significant role in my life, especially in 2011.

Chapter 3

169

169 days before my 50th birthday in 2011, I was on Lundy for my fourth visit.

The journey to the island had lost none of its thrill in the intervening years since my first flight in 2009. In fact, it had taken on an unpredictability that accentuated the sheer joy of arriving. On three of the previous four visits, I had either been unable to get onto the island or to get off the island on the scheduled day, because of adverse weather conditions.

On this occasion, having taken off not only on the scheduled day but also at the scheduled time, my first port of call on arrival was the delightful Marisco Tavern. If you are lucky enough to get on one of the first morning flights from Hartland, you enter the bar area to be faced with up to 40 holidaymakers waiting for their flight off the island. This heightened awareness that your own visit is only just beginning is then enhanced by a good pub lunch and a healthy island walk.

You can take many glorious walks on Lundy and, if you set off from the tavern along the main path, in about 2.5 miles you reach the island's northernmost point.

The scenery changes as you go from the small hamlet through green fields to a landscape that is barren and rugged and almost lunar. For someone who equates 'north' with 'up', the walk has a mildly confusing feel to it. You know you are walking to the north of the island, but at the same time you are gradually going downhill (physically, not metaphorically or mentally!).

On the first afternoon of my latest visit, as I set off on my walk to the north, satiated by my hearty lunch, I found myself slowly decompressing from the work pressures I had left behind on the mainland.

There is something both majestic and therapeutic about walking and thinking. After 2.5 miles of inconsequential musing, along with the gentle rhythmic motion of the exercise and the influence of the lunchtime pint of cider, I began to wonder aimlessly how I could celebrate my upcoming landmark birthday.

Just weeks before, a friend of mine had shared his own 50th birthday plans. He was aiming to do 50 things in his 50th year, with many of them requiring large amounts of adrenalin, finances or alcohol, if not all three at once.

On reaching the most northerly point of the island, I turned to head back up the gentle slope and the passing thoughts of birthday celebrations transformed from mere musings into full-blown focus.

By the time I had retraced my steps to the hub of the village, my friend's idea of '50 things to do' had morphed into a more unconventional but no less ambitious germ of my own birthday celebration idea.

Looking for the perfect location to propagate my thinking, I headed back to the tavern to seek out suitable nutrients and fluids and to start to design my landmark birthday project.

4.9

The Marisco Tavern on an evening is a very different place to the flight-day lunchtime communal waiting room. That evening it was truly charming. Warm, cosy, full of a mixture of transient holidaymakers and island-dwelling locals, it had a ready supply of home-cooked food and a wide-ranging choice of alcoholic beverages.

It also held an additional charm for me, the nostalgia of knowing that my mother and father had held their wedding reception in the very same building and that The Austrian Princess might well, long ago, have bid her fellow taverners goodnight with the tuneful words 'So long, fair well, Auf Wiedersehen, goodbye'. Pet.

Having consumed my evening meal, half a bottle of red wine, and warmed by the fire with no email, phone or human interruptions to bring me back to reality, I started to commit my birthday project to paper.

In the back of my brown leather journal, I scribbled the headlines of the idea that had come to me on my afternoon walk back up the island:

Complete 49 tasks before 4th September (4.9) whilst still 49 years old

Each task must have 4, 9, 49 or 94 as a component part of the task

For me, the creative process of planning something is often much more fun and exciting to do than actually carrying out the plan itself. As a child, during the school week I would love to plan all sorts of carefully considered things to do at the weekend, not bother to do any of them and feel no sense of disappointment.

As I began to consider compiling a list of 49 tasks, I suspect my subconscious was already telling me that I would probably never bother to try to accomplish most of the project, let alone all of it. The indulgent pleasure of simply creating the task list in such a special place was, to me, an end in itself.

For that reason, there was a certain frivolity and carefreeness about the items I included on the list, and I really did not fully appreciate that I would find myself compelled over the next 169* days to complete those 49 items that I randomly chose that night.

'Project 4.9' had begun.

(*Coincidentally, 169 backwards is 9 61, the month (September) and year (1961) of my birth. And, yes, I am a bit of a nerd about birthdays and numbers.)

Quick runs on the board

Chapter 5

Start with 'Why?'

In 2010, a colleague sent me a link to a TED talk. After 18 minutes of watching a rather sexy-looking and sounding American/Englishman called Simon Sinek, I was sold on his idea – Start with 'Why'.

Over the next eight years it became my go-to TED talk when I was working with clients who had not yet seen it and who wanted to develop their leadership skills.

His message was, and still is, simple and easy to follow and the repeated enjoyment of watching and listening to him never waned.

Fast-forward to Lundy.

***

Sitting in the Marisco Tavern with a now-complete list of 49 tasks scribbled in the back of my brown leather-bound journal, I felt that there was no time like the present to start Project 4.9 and attempt my very first task.

I knew that if I was to successfully get a 'quick run on the board', there were a number of factors that I needed to take into consideration when selecting which task to attempt first.

The task needed to be carried out:

- inside the tavern (I really had no desire to leave the womb-like warmth of the bar and go outside)

- in a seated position (I confess, I was already rather drunk after consuming the best part of a bottle of red wine), and

- without fear of injuring or indeed offending any of the other taverners (even in my drunken state, I realised that now was probably not the time to select from the list the item 'Kiss 4 men'; although, in hindsight, it would have got the project and my stay on the island off to an eventful start).

Surveying my freshly inked list, the first task I selected was:

List 49 reasons 'Why' I should do Project 4.9

Whilst it may not be the most exciting of tasks, I'm sure that Simon Sinek would agree that there was indeed no better place to start.

The list I subsequently compiled on that wine-fuelled evening in the warm, dimly lit tavern included 49 random and varied reasons why I should do Project 4.9. The spontaneous reasons included:

- the childish – 'cos I can

- the deep – to find myself

- the OCD – to satisfy my need to make lists (I was already on my second list of the evening)

- the truthful – I'm rather pissed and have no idea

- and the competitive – to do something way more creative and memorable than my mate's '50 things to do in his 50th year'. (At this point, I can hear my therapist mimicking in a Miss Piggy voice 'Competitive? Moi?')

It would be many months before I truly realised the significance of why I had embarked on such an unconventional birthday project. But, for now, the 'Why' list that I had created was sufficient and I was delighted that I had completed Task 1. Only 48 to go.

Chapter 6

Getting off the island

The unpredictability of the weather and consequently the uncertainty of travel on and off Lundy is part of what makes island life so different to everyday mainland life. In a world where so many of us crave a sense of control, there are some things that are simply a law unto themselves.

On 7th August 1954, the day of my parents' wedding, the weather was so bad that my father's best man could not get to the island in time for the ceremony. More than 50 years later, on the morning of my designated departure day, I awoke to an eerie silence broken repeatedly by the faraway sound of a foghorn and to find that the weather holds equal disregard for travel schedules in the twenty-first century as it did in 1954.

Having packed all my belongings into my travel bag, I checked out of The Old School Blue Bungalow where I was staying and made my way to the return flight check-in lounge – aka, the Marisco Tavern. There, I listened for the fourth time to probably the best pre-flight aircraft security briefing you are ever likely to hear, including instructions not to play with any of the dials if you happen to be in the front seat of the helicopter; what to do with your whistle if you end up in the sea, and definitely not to wave goodbye to anyone with your walking poles when standing under the whirling rotor blades.

I then sat waiting for the incoming holidaymakers, who would see me in the same light as I had seen the departing travellers four days earlier.

But they never arrived.

With the island covered by a dense fog that resembled a white eiderdown, and with no prospect of a heavenly laundry change or the fog clearing until mid-afternoon, the announcement came that all flights to and from the island were cancelled for the day and we were told to return the following morning to the same place, same time, for the same pre-flight briefing.

To have been given another 24 hours of freedom on the island was quite literally a gift from heaven.

As I had done on the day of my arrival, I headed north, downhill, and reassured myself that in 2.5 miles, even if the fog had not yet cleared, I would hear the sea crashing on the rocks far below, well before I myself fell off the end of the island and did likewise.

Chapter 7

BAGA Award 4

*Around 70% of our sporting capability is genetic, so if
you want to be good at sport, pick your parents right.*

Year 1 university Sports Science lecture

In my youth, I had been pretty good at sport and, combined
with an ability to rote learn, had managed to get the three
A-level grades required to secure a place at the prestigious
Loughborough University (thanks Mum, thanks Dad, not
only for the genes but for contributing to the university fees
too).

Although my talents lay primarily in the team sports like
netball, hockey and basketball, all Sports Science students
were required to do practical sessions in aesthetic sports
like swimming, dance and gymnastics, during which we
were taught the movement fundamentals by legendary

Loughborough lecturers steeped in the old-fashioned yet timeless values-based ways of teaching.

Of the non-team sports, swimming was definitely not where my aesthetic sporting prowess was best showcased. During our university swimming practical sessions, the finer points of the backstroke, breaststroke or front crawl were simply beyond my physical muscle-memory mastery. I did, however, once artfully and unintentionally remove the trunks of a Northern Irish table tennis international, who was even slower at swimming than me, with a breaststroke leg kick that misfired superbly.

If I was poor at swimming, I was even less talented at contemporary dance. During my four years at Loughborough, I conscientiously practised regularly in nightclubs and parties in the vain hope that alcohol might improve my co-ordination and gracefulness. It didn't.

Gymnastics was the activity where my university aesthetic skills truly peaked.

I have some distant recollection that, quite incredibly, I had been one of the more talented 'gymnasts' in our academic year. (Not to be confused with the Morecambe and Wise 'all the right notes, but not necessarily in the right order' sentence reconstruction that described me as 'an academic and quite incredibly talented gymnast'.)

And so, on a foggy afternoon in March 2011, as I wandered along the footpath to the north of the island on time gifted to me by the weather, my aesthetic past suddenly became my present.

In a parallel universe, I would have been driving along the A361 towards Taunton. But here on Lundy, lost in the moment, with a playful desire to claim a short section of the fog-damp footpath as my private gymnasium, I embarked on Task 2 of Project 4.9.

Do 4 gymnastic moves

The four gymnastic movements selected for Task 2 were significantly influenced by the fact that it had been 26 years, two knee operations and an additional half-stone in weight since I had been an adventurous Loughborough student who threw herself into all things physical.

Despite having once been proficient at simple moves like the flyspring and flick-flack, my Lundy gymnastics more closely resembled moves seen at Tumble Tots.

Whilst some might not instantly equate the roly-poly (aka 'forward roll') with the term 'gymnastic movement', for those of us who attended school PE classes in the 1970s, the forward roll was most certainly up there, on the poster, as one of the movements you had to complete in order to obtain your very own BAGA Gymnastics Award 4 sew-on badge and certificate.

Pretty certain I would be able to accomplish the simple movement, I'd forgotten that, for the last 11 years, I'd suffered intermittently from an inner-ear related dizziness that, under its influence, made me look like I was drunk when I walked and feel like I was hungover when I stopped. It was usually brought on by overtiredness or excess train or plane travel, but that afternoon I found a third trigger for the dizziness. The roly-poly.

The act of the forward roll itself was indeed straight-forward. Squatting on my feet, hands placed on the ground, head tucked in, leaning forward… the slope did the rest.

The ability to stand up afterwards was less straightforward. Not quite sure which way was up (let alone why north was downhill), a short inner-ear rebalancing spreadeagled lie down on the damp grass was required. Once inner-ear equilibrium was achieved, I sat up and, after some consideration, decided I was ready to tackle another gymnastic movement.

My carefully selected second movement was… the backward roll (yes, it was also on the BAGA Gymnastics Award 4 poster).

I do not think there is an equivalent 'roly-poly' nomenclature for the backward roll. Maybe ylop-ylor? Or simply llor? Whatever you call it, a certain level of momentum is required when rolling backwards over your head and hoping to finish on your feet. My first attempt stalled, not quite reaching the critical tipping point and finding myself stuck on the ground on my neck and shoulders, with my rear end in the air. With nearly 11 stone being supported by just a few vertebrae, I wondered whether a 'damaged neck' could soon join 'inner-ear disturbance' as the possible side effects of reattempting the BAGA Gymnastics Award at the age of 49.

With a 180-degree reorientation and now combining downhill momentum in a northerly direction with a little bit more of my long-forgotten youthful energy, attempt number two at the backward roll was a success. I was halfway there on Project 4.9 Task 2.

The third movement was no less technical that the first two – namely the cartwheel. Although successfully completed on first attempt, if it had been judged for its technical merit and artistic presentation, it would not have fared well. Despite my deep dislike of the African violet leotard that we were required to wear for our Loughborough University gymnastics lessons, at that moment on Lundy I began to appreciate just how much more liberating the leotard was for graceful body movement than my somewhat cumbersome outfit of waterproof walking gear, bobble hat, gloves and walking boots. (Thankfully, I had put my walking poles down on the side of the path/gymnasium before attempting the four gymnastic moves.)

And so to the fourth and final gymnastic movement. The headstand. My forte. A move I had successfully mastered first at the tender age of three. At 49, it was completed to near perfection. Perfect balance, forehead delicately positioned on top of a neatly folded (unused) handkerchief (bobble hat now resting on the path alongside the poles), hands positioned equidistant from each other, fingers pointing forwards, toes pointed upwards.

The only thing that stopped me whooping with delight with the completion of Project 4.9 Task 2 was the sound of two fellow fog-delayed walkers who, triggering my rapid transition out of the headstand position, got the surprise of their life as, emerging through the fog, they saw a middle-aged woman in full walking gear sitting in the middle of the damp public footpath next to a bobble hat, a set of walking poles and an (unused) neatly folded handkerchief.

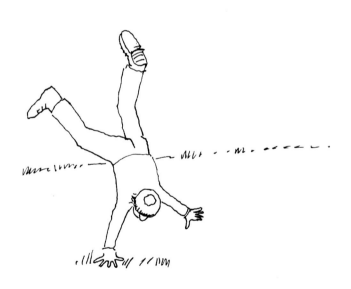

Chapter 8

Thank you, Albert

Following the endorphin high of my afternoon gymnastic endeavours, I returned to the tavern later that night humming the tune of 'Edelweiss', with a Project 4.9 to-do list of 47 items and 167.5 days to complete them in.

For such a small piece of land, Lundy receives a disproportionate amount of attention and radio airtime about its weather. As a result, when those in the know say 'the weather is set fair, you'll be flying home tomorrow', you realise that there is little chance of another fog-delayed day on Lundy and that you will indeed be leaving the Granite Isle and flying back to the mainland the next day.

The realisation that this would be my final evening on the island for some time brought with it a feeling of sadness.

Wanting to spend the last few island hours in my own world of escapism, I revisited my Project 4.9 task list. Looking for something that would meet my own introverted needs and that would not be an incursion into the air space of any of my fellow drinkers, I opted for the following.

Write a list of the 49 most significant people to me

(Have you noticed yet my liking for compiling lists?)

For many years I had been touched by a piece of prose written by Albert Schweitzer in his book *Memoirs of Childhood and Youth*:

> *Another thought moves me when I think back of my youth: that so many people gave me something or were something to me without being aware of it … If those who have become a blessing to us were present with us and if we could tell them how they did, they would be surprised of what flowed from their lives into ours.*

It is a piece of prose that I have given to a very small number of people at significant times in my life, as a way of saying thank you for what had flowed from them to me, without them knowing.

To give myself uninterrupted and dedicated time and space to reflect on those people who 'were something to me' or 'gave me something' was, on that evening, and on that island, deeply satisfying.

Much like the two preceding 'list' tasks, the process was fluid and simple. I sat back in my wooden chair, thought back over my eclectic life, and those that instantly sprang to mind made their way onto the page of my journal.

When I reached 49 names, I realised that my technique for selecting the names was not entirely faultless, as I'd included football icons (who I'd never met) and womanising adulterers (who I unfortunately had), whilst I had not yet listed my parents and siblings.

Being a strict rule follower in my everyday life, with 'be perfect', 'please people' drivers that can be exhausting to live up to (for me and others), I found myself loving the playfulness of Project 4.9. This was my game, with my rules, and when the game is yours, just like a child, you get to change the rules at any time and for any reason you like 😄. (I do wonder what a field hockey Olympic final or soccer World Cup final would be like if each team could call a time-out at some stage in the game and change one of the rules?)

For Task 3, the rule change I decided to add to the original task was simple and straightforward.

Add another 49 significant people to your first list of 49 people

(And make sure you list the significant ones early.)

The heightened focus on ensuring that the really significant people were indeed included in the second half of the list took me into deeper thought. Who had been what to me? And why was what they did so memorable? For the next hour I was lost in my memories.

There was my school friend who would always share half her Twix with me. My gentle godfather who left me, completely unexpectedly, a small sum of money in his will. My first serious boyfriend, who showed me what it was like to be in love and to be loved. The secretary at work who took me under her wing after my mother died and became my surrogate Welsh mother.

As I reread the names, I was humbled to see that many of those who made it onto the list were not linked to me by blood but were people who, at some stage in my life, had offered to me acts of kindness that were small, priceless and unforgettable.

My final night on the island came to an end with three tasks completed and 46 untouched.

As I lay back in the double bed of the Blue Bungalow, I marvelled at the spark of life energy that Project 4.9 and my stay on the island had ignited in me and wondered how long it would remain burning after I left this world of freedom, space and fresh air and flew back to a world where time would speed up and where work would take on a role of disproportionate importance in my life.

Section 3

Mainland Britain activities

Chapter 9

Drive 49 miles

There is a well-known joke about a tourist in Scotland who asks one of the locals for directions to Glasgow. The Scotsman replies: 'Well sir, if I were you, I wouldn't start from here.'

On a crisp fresh morning in late March, a few days after my return from Lundy, my first opportunity to test my mainland Britain commitment to Project 4.9 emerged.

The task I had penned in my brown leather journal, on a warm evening in the Marisco Tavern on Lundy, was a reverse-take on the Scottish joke. Namely, if I were to set off 'from here' and drive for 49 miles, where would I end up?

Drive 49 miles

Having enjoyed Kairos-time (opportune time for action) on Lundy, I was now back in the world of Chronos-time (chronological or sequential time) and so the 'Drive 49 miles' task could no longer be an end in itself but rather it needed to be seamlessly and intentionally integrated into the fee-paying work of my day.

My destination later that morning was the beautiful capital city of Cardiff in south Wales, where I had lived for seven eventful and impressionable years and where I was due for a business meeting.

Setting off from my Gloucestershire home, my plan was that, wherever I was on my Cardiff-bound journey, when I hit 49 miles, I would stop the car and mark the event in some significant and unique way.

Setting my journey milometer to zero, I reversed out of the driveway and set off up Church Road in the direction of south Wales.

The hypnotic nature of mile after mile after mile of relentless A40/M50/A449 dual carriageway and the familiarity of the route meant that my mind soon wandered off into a flow-like state. If anyone (other than the traffic police) had asked me what I had seen along the route I would have struggled to answer.

At around 45 miles from Gloucester, I remembered with a start my Project 4.9 intention and, with my 49-mile end point speeding towards me in less than five minutes, I began seeing the road and surrounding countryside from a new, narrowing perspective. I realised that I was facing the very real prospect that when my milometer hit 49 miles I may well have to pull over onto the hard shoulder and feign a breakdown just to achieve my task.

And then, as the milometer clicked onto 48, a square blue-and-grey sign covered in the grime of highway traffic appeared on the roadside. 'P 1 mile'.

With a childlike smile and a reminder of the energy rush that had been sparked on Lundy after I had completed the first three tasks, a mile later I looked in the mirror, signalled left and manoeuvred off the dual carriageway into the awaiting layby.

In a spontaneous celebration that was befitting of the level of challenge of the task itself, I got out of the car, ran round it once and, in my own Formula 1-style celebration, cracked open a can of Diet Coke that had been rolling around the footwell of the car, inadvertently spraying both myself and the car with warm, fizzy, sticky brown liquid.

To this day, that layby holds a very special place in my heart and, as if it has taken on a personality of its own, regularly receives a special queenly wave from me as I drive past. When there is actually a car parked there, I often receive a tentative wave back from the inhabitants who, seeing a fifty-something woman grinning broadly and waving their way, make the assumption she must be known to them, as who else would she be waving at?

Chapter 10

Looking up

For ten months of my life, I dated a birdwatcher. Every day, he would meticulously and religiously record the birds he had observed, coding them, cross-checking them against previous months and years, and logging them manually with a blunt pencil in a well-thumbed and grubby A4 exercise book.

His talent was not just recognising the birds by sight, but also recognising them just as easily from their call (although I could only take his word for it).

I have never been out with a trainspotter or cricket scorer, but I suspect there is a similarity in the underlying personality traits that draw people to such fastidious pursuits and record-keeping hobbies.

Quite early on in our relationship, around the time we started sharing en-suite hotel rooms, we were staying in a small hotel on the outskirts of Ross-on-Wye in rural Herefordshire.

Early one morning, with the toilet door and window both open, he was sitting down doing his business when he broke wind. Within seconds came a voice from the bathroom: 'Did you hear that? A red woodpecker!' Somewhat surprised by both the uninhibited flatulence and then the follow-up comment, I mistakenly thought that he had taken up the hobby of attempting to imitate birds with flatulence and was proudly alerting me to the skills of his red woodpecker impersonation. The mundane reality was that he was asking me whether I too had heard the real woodpecker call through the open bathroom window.

Although I may not have been able to recognise the sound of the red woodpecker that early morning, (just as the sun was rising) in Herefordshire, I did have a fairly good knowledge of birds compared to many of my close friends. My father had been a keen birdwatcher and so I had been brought up to recognise the buzzard, peregrine falcon, red kite and choughs that we would see on our west Wales holidays, as well as the common garden birds that pecked at our milk bottle tops, lived in our eaves and serenaded us at dawn and dusk in our Gloucestershire home.

But logging birds daily – I just did not get it. Where was the excitement in that? I was soon to find out.

Spot and correctly identify 49 different species of birds

Of all the tasks in Project 4.9, this was the one that most significantly changed how I looked at the world. Between April and August of 2011, my outlook altered. I looked at the sky, I looked at the trees, I looked in the hedgerows and I looked at lakes, rivers and ponds. It was quite literally an eye-opening experience, and I was truly sorry when it was over and the task had been completed.

During those five months, I spotted and correctly identified sea birds, garden birds, woodland birds, birds in the UK and birds in the USA. But of all the 49 birds that I spotted and identified correctly, there was one that was special to me.

Anyone who walks regularly through Hyde Park in London will have seen the plethora of different birds that inhabit the water and land around the Serpentine lake.

On an early morning walk from Paddington station to Hyde Park Corner, I noticed a distinctive duck waddling along the pavement next to the lake. Whilst it was clear that this was a new bird for my list, I did not know what it was called. 'Duck' seemed such an insult to such an arrogant-looking bird. So, in the period before it was correctly identified, the duck was gendered 'he' and affectionately given the name Donald.

Seizing the opportunity to capture the evidence of 'spotting' Donald, I took out my brick of a mobile phone, photographed 'him' and saved the image to show my father when I next saw him (this was before the time of sending photographs over the internet).

The following weekend I had the opportunity to share my photograph with my father. Even at the age of 49, I still found it a strange experience when he did not have an answer to all my questions. But Donald (the duck) was unrecognisable to Donald (the father). He had no idea who he was (the duck, not my father).

What followed was a serendipitous return to childhood. Together, my father and I leafed through garden bird books looking for Donald (not there) and then *The Readers Digest Book of British Birds* (not there).

Finally, we had to resort to the internet. Searching for 'duck, grey, orange' in Images, we were faced with a colourful array of pictures of succulent-looking duck in orange sauce and photos of mallards. But no Donald. With an inspired yet subtle switch of the word 'duck' to 'goose' – there he was, a picture of our very own Donald – and his species – an Egyptian goose. (Tick – Donald had been spotted and correctly identified.)

Birdwatching was such a great task to complete. To my flatulent ex-boyfriend, I'd like to thank you for the inspiration.

To bird watchers and 'twitchers' everywhere, I salute and respect your endeavours so much more now that my eyes have been opened to your world.

To fellow record-keeping hobbyists like trainspotters and cricket scorers, I'm afraid I've still got some way to go to understand your passion.

Chapter 11

The collage

When I was four, I thought every family had an Uncle Ernie.

A towering colossus of a man built like a barn door, with hands the size of shovels, he had a ruddy complexion and a silver horseshoe of hair that reminded me of Santa Claus.

He wasn't a blood relative, but he was part of the Mayes family fabric, his existence marked by his intermittent visits to Fairlawn, the family home, and, annually, by the arrival of a large and colourful RNLI Christmas card.

Ernie had long since faded into the background of my life until my first visit to Lundy brought him fully back into focus.

Lundy has three lighthouses and between 1953 and 1954, when my mother and father first met and then married,

Ernie was one of the lighthouse keepers and figures in their wedding photographs.

I love the fact that their special friendship remained intact long after my parents last visited the island and long after Ernie was made redundant, along with all lighthouse keepers around the world as their lighthouses became fully automated.

I cannot remember when the Christmas cards from Uncle Ernie stopped arriving. But stories about him remained part of our shared family history.

One of his more memorable visits to the family home was in his brand-spanking-new MGBGT car. In an event that was wrong on many levels, he took my brother Dave and me (aged 9 and 4 respectively) for a drive in his two-seater MG, without seatbelts, along the new A40 Golden Valley bypass between Cheltenham and Gloucester. Dave was in the front seat and I was somehow squeezed onto the back window ledge/shelf. With the wind howling in through the fully opened triangular window, I was just able to see over my brother's shoulder as the black-and-red needle passed the 100mph marker on the round silver-rimmed Smith's speedometer.

Uncle Ernie came back into my memory more significantly in 2009. A few days after I'd returned from my first Lundy visit, I was gushing about my visit to a colleague. Infected by my enthusiasm, he said he had a book I might like to read that he would send to me. True to his word, two days later I received a package through the post and inside it was a hardback copy of a book called *Stargazing: Memoirs of a Young Lighthouse Keeper*.

Stargazing is a beautiful story and an absorbing read. Written by Peter Hill, it is what it says on the cover – the memoirs of a young lighthouse keeper and, as described by the publishers, 'a charming and beautifully written memoir that is not only a heartfelt lament for Hill's own youth and innocence but also for a simpler and more honest age'.

Through Peter Hill's story and words, I was able to imagine what Uncle Ernie's life as a lighthouse keeper on Lundy might have been like all those years ago.

I loved Peter Hill's book, not just because of its compelling story, and the way it captured my imagination, but also because of its dustcover illustration, an artist's impression of a tower lighthouse rising from a blackened hillside on a starry night. The beam of light from the top of the lighthouse illuminates the lower cloud-filled sky, which gradually darkens to a jet-black canvas punctuated by hundreds of tiny, white, starlike specks.

Each time I looked at the cover, it had the time-travel capacity to transport me back to Lundy.

The colourful connection between Lundy, Ernie and lighthouses thus became the inspiration on that warm March evening in the Marisco Tavern on Lundy, when I added this Project 4.9 task.

Make a collage of the covers of your 9 favourite books

The thoughtful process of selecting my nine favourite books was relatively easy; the making of the collage less so. Although I owned all the books I listed in the task, I had to buy new copies of many of them so that, in an act that felt like vandalism, I could remove their covers and arrange them artistically in a collage.

The collage included the colourful covers of *The Book Thief*, *The Time Traveler's Wife*, *The English Patient*… and, in an act that felt like my very own game of *Tetris*, I turned nine multi-sized covers into a perfectly frameable rectangle.

Of all the nine favourite books whose covers made it onto the collage, Peter Hill's *Stargazing* was, without doubt, the centrepiece and, for me, what truly defied the saying 'never judge a book by its cover' – both book and cover are truly mesmerising.

Chapter 12

Dish 49

In the late 1960s, Britain was not the colourful, multicultural culinary nation it is today. A rare window into the food of others came from the resident TV chef Fanny Cradock and her husband Johnnie (what a great pair of names). Fanny was to subtlety like a bull is to a china shop and, as an impressionable ten-year-old girl with no real interest in cooking, I was more captivated by her animated eyebrows and over-the-top make up than her culinary creations; and Johnnie's reputed infamous line ('May all your doughnuts turn out like Fanny's') would have passed well and truly over my head.

My culinary experiences first ventured overseas when a cardboard box of Vesta chow mein with crispy noodles arrived in our kitchen. The pre-cut pieces of a dried pasta-like substance, a suspicious brown 'sauce mix' powder and brittle yellow strips of who-knows-what combined miraculously with hot water and boiling oil to produce what I thought to be my first 'foreign meal'.

There is a Chinese proverb that the fish is the last to know that it is swimming in water. Little did I realise that at that time I was that carp. Throughout my childhood, I had been exposed to 'foreign' food on a weekly basis. My Austrian mother (who, like many wives and mothers of that era, did all the cooking) was well skilled at camouflaging Austrian food under a non-threatening easily pronounceable English pseudonym.

English	Austrian
Meat in breadcrumbs	Wiener schnitzel
Thinly sliced cucumber in vinegar	Gurkensalat
Red stew	Hungarian goulash
Cooked apple in pastry	Apfelstrudel
Shortbread biscuits	Kipfel

At a time when money was tight and mouths plentiful, 'eating out' in the Mayes family was restricted to birthdays or the arrival of a significant visitor like Uncle Ernie, or friends and relatives from overseas. But somewhere between the cardboard Vesta experience and getting dressed up to go out for a meal came the arrival to rural Gloucestershire of the first Chinese and Indian 'takeaways'.

When my mother brought home our first curry in the early 1970s, I remember my father's horror at the disruption to the Saturday status quo and the fact that the familiar lunchtime regulars of toad in the hole and macaroni cheese (with boiled eggs) were being benched in favour of a far more colourful Asian dish that left permanent yellow stains on the kitchen worktop.

Within a year of our first curry, Chinese and Indian restaurants opened in all the local towns and cities and, soon after, the village of Churchdown, Gloucestershire, had its very own Chinese takeaway.

The menu, although written in English, was like a foreign language. Most of the words we really didn't understand. It took regular and deliberate practice (plus a few mistakes) for the Mayes family to find out what they liked and, with a number that became as memorable as the telephone numbers of the local doctor, chemist and window cleaner, 26, 43, 59 (and egg fried rice) became our standard order.

And so it was to this very takeaway that I returned to complete one of my Project 49 tasks.

Select from any menu dish number 49

The idea of this task was to be that little bit more adventurous when visiting a restaurant or takeaway. Instead of resorting to type, studiously poring over a restaurant menu, asking everyone else what they were having, salivating at the multitude of different choices, and then playing safe and ordering what I always ordered, this particular task required me to select item number 49 from any menu, without reading the menu first.

On my last Friday night as a 49-year-old, I was back in the village of Churchdown. With less than 24 hours left before I turned 50, I walked out of the house, across the familiar back lawn where I had first learned to cycle, through the old wooden back gate that was older than me and set off up Church Road to The Golden City.

You can actually see the takeaway from the back garden gate, so the trek there and back burned up fewer calories than those inhaled whilst waiting in line for my chance to order.

With great anticipation and excitement of what menu item number 49 would serve up, I scanned the menu, ordered the item (plus egg fried rice) and trekked back down Church Road to the sanctuary of my home and my Friday night meal.

Deepak Chopra and many other wise people talk of mindfulness and food, encouraging you to pay attention to what you are eating. They tell you to eat in silence, away from the blare of the TV that often distracts you from the true experience of tasting and appreciating your food.

Many meals I have eaten before and since have been beautiful creations, explosions of taste or quite simply a much-needed satiation of hunger. But this one was special.

The meal was eaten in silence and solitude, whilst sitting in the family kitchen that had survived two fires, four children, five dogs and one cat; at the table where I had observed the dynamics of family interactions that would serve me well in my later career, learned the strange Austro-English etiquette of table manners and courted my first serious boyfriend.

For its simplicity, setting and significance, there are few meals that will ever be more memorable or poignant to me.

And the dish itself?

Squid in a jus of butternut squash with mussels and prawns.

As if! This was a village takeaway in rural Gloucestershire in 2011.

Golden City dish number 49 was beef with fresh tomato (plus egg fried rice).

Section 4

Central Europe activities

Chapter 13

The promise

In May 1993, I first met my Austrian cousin Lotte and her son Sven.

I was living in Cardiff at the time, and the invitation had come from my mother, suggesting that I return home to Gloucestershire to meet them whilst they were staying in our family home, Fairlawn.

I found Sven and Lotte Budik sitting beside each other on the old family couch in the living room, speaking animated German to my mother.

I was captivated. Not only by the language and the animation, but especially by Sven. I kept thinking how much Hitler would have liked this blue-eyed blond Arian youth and whether a relationship with my cousin's son would be out of the question? None of this I voiced out loud at the time; it didn't seem appropriate to share thoughts of

Hitler or questions about incest with people you'd only just met.

Sven and Lotte were staying with my mother for a few days so that they could visit the Badminton Horse Trials and various other horse-related meetings.

Though I didn't know it at the time of their visit, my mother would be dead within the year from cancer. It is with some certainty that I now realise that she knew she had not long on this earth, and she had orchestrated invitations to the family home for all four of the Mayes siblings so that we would each have the chance to meet our Austrian relatives whilst they were staying in Churchdown.

For the 12 years following my mother's death, the relationship between the Mayes family and the Budik family was sustained by Christmas cards, occasional wedding invitations and christening photographs.

And then, in 2005, my sister and I made our first visit to Vienna together. With the families reunited, Lotte shared that one of the last things my mother had asked of her when she was in Churchdown was to promise to keep the connection between the family in Austria and us, her four children.

From that year onwards I was drawn magnetically to the Budik family.

The fulfilment of the promise and the relationship I have with my Austrian relatives has been a gift. It has brought a colour to the edges of my life that makes it so much more expansive.

For me as a German speaker with a tiny vocabulary, the Budiks present a safe space to explore the challenge of being understood and misunderstood without fear of ridicule. To play a game of guessing the meaning of German and English words and to marvel at their ability to know the English words for terms I struggle to spell. They provide the opportunity to explore the ways in which humour translates across countries, cultures and families.

My relationship with my Austrian relatives also highlights that everyday life for some people is completely alien to others.

Many of my lasting memories from my childhood are of the four siblings and two parents sitting and talking together as a family around the big, square wooden kitchen table. This was long before the advent of sitting in front of the TV with dinner on a tray.

When my sister and I visited the Austrian family in 2005, we were transported back into that familiar space of eating as (an extended) family around the kitchen table.

The Budik family, like the Mayes family, had a set of unspoken table manners. You could leave the table when the meal was over and you were invited to do so. If for some reason you needed to leave the table early, you would politely ask permission of your meal-table companions, giving a reason for doing so.

The manners were the same. But one of my first meals in their family home gave me a real appreciation that mealtimes with the horse-loving Budiks always held the possibility of being slightly different.

In early August 2007, we were sitting around the Austrian family kitchen table, in full conversation. We had just finished the main course of Lotte's traditional wiener schnitzel and gurkensalat and had decided to take a breather before the dessert (or *nachtisch*). Our Austrian family are great lovers of their food, and great cooks too. So, desserts are especially significant to them, and us, and not something to be missed.

Without warning, one of my cousins, who was a vet, stood up, apologised and asked to be excused from the table. With a sentence I had not heard before at a family meal table (nor, in fact, since) she explained, 'Please excuse me, I have to go and artificially inseminate a horse', and, without pausing for a response, continued, 'I will be back in time for the dessert'.

My vivid imagination was in overdrive. Even if I had been fluent enough to translate what I was thinking, this was one time that I think the humour would have been lost in translation. All I could think was, 'You will wash your hands, won't you?'

From 2005 to the current day, I return annually to my motherland to honour my heritage and connect with my cousins. Family mealtimes continue to be bountiful and entertaining, and the bits in between are pretty special too.

And so, in the summer of 2011, I was delighted to be able to complete a small number of my Project 4.9 tasks in a country that is very, very dear to me.

Chapter 14

Viennese biathlon

For as long as I can remember I have always had a bicycle. Not the same one. Various bikes befitting my age, body size, leg length and pocket money.

My childhood memories involving cycling are varied. On the back lawn for the first time without stabilisers. The four Mayes children cycling behind our mother on the main road through our quiet Gloucestershire village, with her screeching in her German accent that she was the mother duck and we were her little ducklings. Crashing into a stationary car on an unlit country road and bending the two front forks of my bike, as well as giving the (presumably not married to each other) kissing couple in the back seat the fright of their lives.

And then, in the summer of 2009, I fell in love with a KTM. KTM is an Austrian manufacturer of motorcycles and bicycles (other brands are available).

2009 was the first year that I hired a bike for the full two weeks of my Austrian summer holiday. At the end of the rental period, the hire company offered an unexpected deal. For a few extra euros I could purchase the bike I had been hiring, as long as I took it away there and then and did not require the hire company to ship it anywhere or do anything but issue a receipt.

And so, I took ownership of my first KTM and entered into an annual routine of keeping it wintered in my cousin Lotte's garden shed 15 miles from Vienna (the rest of her house was there too, not just her shed). Each year, I would return in the summer, lovingly hose it down (the bike, not the shed) and give the tyres *luft* before pedalling away into the sunflower-lined roads of Lower Austria.

It was somewhat inevitable, given the constant presence of bicycles in my life, that a cycling-related task was going to feature in Project 4.9, and what better place to complete it than in Austria?

Cycle 49 miles

Austria may well be renowned for its mountains and hills that are alive with the sound of music. Less well known are its fantastic flat cycle paths, perfect for those who see no point whatsoever in pedalling hard up some ridiculously steep mountain only to come down the other side, shit-scared of falling off.

Austria is one of five countries through which Euro Cycle Route 6 passes on its way from the west of France, through major cities such as Passau, Vienna, Bratislava, Budapest and Bucharest, and on to the Black Sea. There is a 20-mile stretch between the Austrian towns of Krems and Melk where the cycle path follows the banks of the Danube before turning inland to meander through tiny villages, vineyards and nostalgic towns with ruined castles. The surrounding scenery is simply stunning.

Whilst years later I would cycle 80 miles in a day along this scenic route with no problem, in 2011 the longest distance I had ever cycled was around 20 miles, so hills or no hills (with or without live music), my project task of cycling 49 miles was going to take me into uncharted territory.

The cycle ride that I undertook for my project started outside the family flat where I was staying in the 4th District of Vienna. Unlike my very first mainland task (driving 49 miles and seeing where I ended up), the cycling task was carefully planned. There were two conditions: it had to end back at the family flat and it had to take in a specific, predetermined section of the River Danube.

To get to the river from the flat involved cycling around the famous Ringstrasse (where Hitler paraded Nazi tanks in 1938 to celebrate Austria being *anschlussed* or 'annexed' by Germany), over one of the many small bridges that cross the Danube Canal, along the famous treelined Prater Hauptallee (where Kipchogee broke the two-hour marathon record in 2019) and then across another bridge onto the Donauinsel – a long thin (renovated) island in the middle of the not-so-blue Danube. This small cycle-track-covered island was to be the location of 40 miles of the 49-mile ride.

Living in a landlocked country with no natural coastline, the Austrians' ability to be resourceful with the meeting of land and water (be that a lake, river or swimming pool) is an amazing and colourful sight. The Austrians are also – and this is a huge generalisation (as I cannot vouch for Gustav Klimt, Arnold Schwarzenegger or indeed Hitler) – naturist sun-lovers. On a sunny summer's day, on certain sections of the banks of the Danube, there are more naked bodies on display than in the full back catalogues of magazines like *Mayfair* or *Penthouse*.

Being aware of this fact, one of the conditions of my 49-mile cycling task was that the route had a carefully researched, predetermined midpoint destination in the famous 'naturist' section of the Danube. This was not for some voyeuristic reasons, but rather it gave me the opportunity to combine two Project 4.9 tasks in the same day and to complete my very own Austrian biathlon.

Swim 49 strokes with no clothes on

In common with rivers in many other central European countries, the Danube's banks feature robust pontoons jutting out so that, when the weather is sunny long enough and reliably enough, whole families can sit together and bob up and down as the wake of a passing boat produces waves unconnected to the wind, moon or tide.

The pontoons are designed with ample space to stretch out, sunbathe and then slip effortlessly into the water to cool off. Often, several groups of naked people, unknown to each other, will share a pontoon; respecting each other's privacy in a non-voyeuristic fashion.

Given the nature of the task I was hoping to accomplish, and my own English prudishness, it was important to me to find an uninhabited pontoon if I was to get my kit off and attempt my 49 strokes of nude swimming.

Thankfully, on the day I had chosen for this adventure the ambient temperature was just below the threshold that triggered a mass-migration of flaccid body parts to the Danube riverbank and so I wheeled my bike onto an uninhabited pontoon and started to disrobe.

I think in my imagination I was going to dive perfectly into the water, no ripples to be seen and all body parts beautifully aligned. In reality, I made a slightly less dignified entry, tentatively climbing down the set of metal steps attached to the river side of the pontoon, with my 49-year-old rear end protruding ungracefully.

The 49 doggie-paddle strokes that followed were exhilarating, refreshing and liberating (if not particularly aesthetically attractive). The combined nervous excitement of exposing myself to the Austrian public and the immersion into what was deceptively cold water had a distinct physiological impact on me. Not only did my heart race and my breath catch, but my nipples stood to attention as if they thought they were taking part in the 2011 Blue Danube wet t-shirt competition – but without the t-shirt. I loved the experience (the swim, not the wet t-shirt bit). It was one of my favourite sensory-filled moments of the 169-day project.

Task completed, I climbed back up the cool metal steps to find to my horror that the pontoon was no longer unoccupied. A naked man of maturing years, judging by his wrinkles at my eye line, was now standing at the top of the steps waiting to enter the water using the same route I was using to exit.

I had heard that, when people who don't know each other at all or very well find themselves naked in front of each other, a good strategy is the 'Exocet Missile' technique – to lock eyes with the other person and not let the gaze wander. Not something I had had much practice in, but now was my chance to unexpectedly test out the interesting theory.

My ability to comprehend the German language at the best of times is pretty poor (I got a Grade U (unclassified) in my German O-Level), but when the blood that was meant to go to your brain to help with mental word-processing has redistributed itself to your cheeks (both sets) and you are standing opposite an unknown naked man whilst intensely staring into his eyes, the Anglo-Austrian exchange to follow was always going to be challenging.

He made three attempts to engage me in German conversation, all of which went unanswered.

Finally, in a pigeon-English sentence, which indicated that my Exocet technique had clearly not locked and engaged quickly enough to keep his eyes from wandering chestward, he said: 'The water. It must be very, very cold.'

My cycle ride back to the flat was relatively uneventful. Given my depleted energy resources and the fact that the final two miles was mostly uphill, I smiled politely at the numerous tourists who, heading to the famous Belvedere Palace, overtook me on foot.

The flat in which I was staying had been the home of my great-grandmother, and we have a family picture of my mother, aged four (circa 1925), sitting in the sunshine on the front doorstep. The flat is on the top floor of a classic old building in a street called Belvedergasse; if you lean far enough out, you can actually see the famous Belvedere Palace from the two bedroom windows.

Arriving back in Belvedergasse, one mile short of the 49 miles, I cycled repeatedly up and down a short stretch of the one-way street until the milometer clicked onto the desired end figure. Dismounting, then securely locking the bike to the bike stand, I stepped over the threshold where my mother had sat over 80 years ago, and I climbed with weary legs the 113 concrete steps that took me to the fourth-floor apartment.

Collapsing, totally exhausted, on the bed, with a body that was being flooded with post-exercise hormones and memories from the day, I found myself feeling absolutely elated at my two-task achievement, and also, unexpectedly and rather unnervingly, slightly horny.

Chapter 15

The tram

My childhood years were spent living midway between Cheltenham and Gloucester. I often told people that I was the '&' in the C&G (Cheltenham and Gloucester) Building Society, and even, nostalgically, invested my first ISA savings allowance in a C&G ISA.

In my teenage years, sometime between the age when I was allowed to go shopping on my own and before I could drive, if I wanted to go to either of the towns I would catch the 547, 548 or 549 bus. (Many years later, they got renumbered in my mind to 47, 48 and 49.)

Bus travel didn't suit me well. I had the capacity to feel motion sick at just the thought of it, and the act itself was no better. But by the time I had reached the tender age of 49, I had grown out of the habit (of both feeling sick and catching buses to Cheltenham or Gloucester).

However, I'm sure these early evocative memories were somehow tapped into on the warm March evening in the Marisco Tavern on Lundy, when I added:

Take the first bus number 49 that you see

to the Project 4.9 list.

Maybe there was some hidden romantic notion of spotting the number 49 to Cheltenham, climbing up onto the top deck, humming Cliff Richard's melody 'We're all going on a summer holiday' and reliving part of my youth, but without the aid of a sick bag.

The first number 49 bus that I spotted and rode was not, however, in romantic Gloucestershire and was not a bus at all.

Given that many of the European cities I visited during the summer of 2011 had an array of different kinds of public transport, I had decided that a change to the rules of the project was in order for added excitement, and that buses and trams were both valid transport options for this particular task in Project 4.9.

The result of this slight modification to the rules of the game meant that Hungary was the location for completion of this particular task.

I was in Budapest with three of my Austrian relatives and my sister. At the time, the Austrians were not aware of Project 4.9, but my sister was. It was our second day of three and we were walking down the main shopping street in the city. Talking about whatever Austro-English topic was entertaining us at the time, I looked round to see a tram approaching from behind. There, above the front window (windscreen), was a square plaque with the number 49 clearly displayed. With no idea where the tram was heading and no time to explain my behaviour to my Austrian relatives, I ran to the tram stop a few yards ahead, flagged it down and climbed on board.

The tram took off up the street, leaving my relatives bewildered as I gleefully waved them goodbye. In what could have been no more than 300 yards (and just enough time to pay for the ticket), the tram's momentum changed from a strained acceleration uphill to a gentle deceleration until it slowed to a stop. With my relatives still clearly in sight, I stepped off the tram, said a heartfelt 'thank you' to the driver (and the tram) and walked energetically back down the street to join them.

The fact that they did not seem to need an explanation for my unusual behaviour, picking up the pre-49 tram ride conversation with seamless ease, made the ride all the more memorable (after all, this was a family who inseminated horses between the first and second course of a meal).

Chapter 16

Buy a painting

In 2005, Malcolm Gladwell's book *Blink: The Power of Thinking Without Thinking* presented 'research from psychology and behavioural economics on the mental processes that work rapidly and automatically from relatively little information'.

In his book, Gladwell tells a story of the Getty kouros, which was a statue brought to the J. Paul Getty Museum in California. It was thought by many experts to be legitimate, but when others first looked at it, their initial responses were sceptical. The authenticity of the kouros is still unproven and Gladwell's book explored in some detail the significance of noticing our first impressions.

My memory of this story was that, subsequent to the Getty kouros story, one museum curator asked his staff that, if ever they had a new piece of art they wanted to show him to test its authenticity, they should surprise him with it – that is, hide it somewhere where he would suddenly find it (for instance, in his locker at work or in a toilet cubicle). That way, he felt he could truly test his intuitive response to first seeing it, rather than be primed consciously beforehand.

On an unexpected wet and windy August morning in 2011, I was flip-flopping my way through the puddles on one of the cobbled streets of Vienna. The street radiates out from the main Fiaker-filled Hofberg area. The rainwater was carrying with it small brownish-yellow remnants of horse excrement and straw, as a result of which my concentration was finely focused on my foot placement.

This particular street has a small number of artists' shops that I had previously visited. Entering one of the shops and reassured by the dry land underfoot, my gaze lifted slowly to take in a large picture that dominated the top half of the shop wall.

The visceral reaction to the image happened in a split second – eyes, brain, stomach churn, tear ducts all sending synchronous signals. I was caught completely off guard, captivated by the composition, and was surprised to find myself crying.

Buy a painting worth more than £94

As part of Project 4.9, I had set myself the task of buying a piece of art worth more than £94. The sum was set to encourage me to buy something a little bit more significant than my usual mass-produced prints or over-enlarged photographs.

I loved the picture that had induced such an instinctive response in me. Transfixed by it, I could not work out how I could possibly afford such a picture (well over £94 and outside my pocket money limit), let alone get it home on a budget airline.

In a slightly stunned state, I left the shop and splashed unconsciously through the brown-and-yellow puddles back to the family flat where, reunited with my sister, I shared my 'Blinklike' experience. My sister reassured me that, if I really wanted the picture, she would loan me the money and, judging by the gift she had received from our father for her own 50th birthday some years previously, it was likely that I would receive a similar amount for mine – enough to pay her back for the picture.

I thought about the picture all night. With the next day being our final day in Austria, I took a final opportunity to return to the shop and recalibrate my response.

On entering the small shop, I took one look at the picture and instantly felt a familiar churn in my stomach and tears on my cheeks. The same thing had happened again.

My visceral response to this evocative picture was like a perfect storm of memories. Memories from various stages of my life that were unconscious most of the time until they collided and were brought to my awareness in a small art shop on Josephsplatz in Vienna.

The perfect storm had two distinctive parts.

Perfect Storm Part 1

On the first day of every year, my mother spent part
of the morning tuning into the New Year's Day concert
from Vienna. My earliest memories of the event were of
her listening to the broadcast on the radio and then, as
telecommunications improved, it made its way into our
sitting room first in black and white and then in glorious
technicolour, courtesy of BBC Two.

A tradition of the two-part concert is that the encore
includes the twin delights of 'The Blue Danube' waltz and
the 'Radetzky March' – two distinctly different pieces of
music, but equally evocative. The first starts with a long,
drawn-out note that is instantly recognisable to anyone
with even a passing knowledge of classical music, worthy
of a 'I'll name that tune in one' reaction. The latter has
a symbol-crashing start and a foot-tapping repetitive
rhythm that is impossible to sit still to (at least, if you are a
member of either the Mayes family or the New Year's Day
Musikverein Concert Hall audience).

As the years passed after my mother's death, the tradition
of watching the New Year's Day concert became part of my
own annual ritual, as a mark of remembrance to her and my
Austrian heritage, with the encore by far my favourite part
of the musical programme.

The 'Radetzky March' would traditionally include audience-
participation, where the conductor would interact with the
animated concertgoers, encouraging them (and me) to clap
quietly then loudly at various parts of the piece.

The more melodic 'Blue Danube' was often accompanied by beautiful video footage of the castles, monasteries, vineyards, villages and towns that lined the banks of the majestic river.

The significance of the video footage took on an altogether different magnitude after the summer of 2008, the year I sailed on the blue Danube for the very first time.

When I say 'sailed', I use the term loosely. I was actually on board a mid-sized steamship/ferry, together with my sister and hundreds of other passengers, being expertly steered by a ship's captain.

The day trips that sail up and down the Danube start in Krems, 50 miles east of Vienna. The boats make short stops in tiny, picturesque towns like Dürnstein (where Richard the Lionheart was imprisoned) before docking at the town of Melk for a short while before heading back down the river to Krems.

If you don't look up, Melk is like many of the other small Danube riverside towns. A small number of cobbled streets are filled with cafés and shops selling postcards, apricot jam, apricot brandy, pictures of apricots, pictures of apricot blossom and calendars with pictures of towns selling apricots.

But when you look up, there above you is a massive, magnificent Benedictine abbey.

Yellow-and-white brick walls rise out of the cliff face on the hill behind the town houses, with a pair of marzipan-looking turrets rising even higher above the 497 rooms and 1,365 windows of the Abbey.

Its sheer size cannot be fully appreciated from the cobbled town below, and the best way to discover its magnificence is from the range of postcards that capture it from every angle.

There are many beautiful sights along the river with the potential to feature in the New Year's Day concert video footage that accompanies the 10 minutes of Johann Sebastian Strauss's 'Blue Danube' – old castles, quaint villages, trellised hillside vineyards; not to mention the less favourable sights of the nudist beaches. But, if there ever was a compilation of the 'top 10 sights', Melk Abbey, in all its yellow-and-white dignity, would be right up there, instantly recognisable from any angle.

(The nudist beaches have never yet made it into any BBC Two footage.)

Perfect Storm Part 2

Much as I had grown up eating Austrian food without realising it, I had also lived in a family house adorned with Austrian art. The Austro-Hungarian artist Luigi Kasimir was a favourite of my mother's. His famous coloured etchings include landmarks of Vienna, landscapes from the Austrian countryside and other world sights, including New York city skyscrapers and Yosemite Park. It is reported that one of his pictures hung on the wall of Sigmund Freud's consulting room in Vienna.

Kasimir (senior) died around the time of my birth, but his son Robert continued in his father's footsteps, utilising similar ground-breaking techniques to produce equally attractive and colourful etchings.

Following in my own mother's footsteps, I continued to seek out Kasimir (junior) etchings and for my first few visits to Vienna they became the go-to Christmas gift to my three siblings, especially once I had found a small shop on the Mariahilfestrasse that sold the delightful etchings in sizes suitable for hand-luggage suitcases (and prices suitable for a modest monthly pay packet).

By the time of my 49th birthday, all the Mayes siblings could genuinely start a sentence, if desired but I believe never used: 'You must come up and see my Austrian etching sometime.'

Perfect Storm Part 1 + Part 2

And so it was, when I flip-flopped into the little art shop in Vienna, on the penultimate day of my 2011 summer holiday, the painting that took my breath away as I looked up at the wall was a 16 x 20-inch signed Kasimir (junior) etching of the stunning Melk Abbey, drawn from a vantage point on the banks of the river Danube.

I could think of no way to get such a large item on EasyJet without incurring ridiculous excess luggage costs. So, with a heavy heart and a final glance back at the picture, I left the shop in the sure knowledge that my search for a £94+ picture would have to start again.

In the weeks that followed my return to the UK from my Austrian summer holiday, I often thought of the etching, and no matter how many art galleries and art shops I visited I could find nothing that evoked in me such an emotional response.

With only a few days to go before my 50th birthday, I was getting desperate to complete this particular task.

Of course, at some level I knew that Kasimir art was known outside of Vienna (after all, there were at least five pieces in various Mayes houses in Gloucestershire). And even though internet shopping was relatively new to me at that time, and I had purchased many Austrian things on the internet, the thought of finding a piece of Austrian art on the web was deeply buried in my subconscious.

Whatever it was that triggered the idea of googling 'Kasimir etchings' the week before my birthday, the outcome was beyond my expectations. There, hidden among hundreds of images, was the picture I had fallen in love with in Vienna.

In a flurry of online activity, I purchased the frameless picture for more than £94, but well below the price of the sister copy in Vienna.

The picture arrived from America a few weeks after my 50th birthday, and with the money my father had given me as my birthday gift I took great pleasure in having it beautifully and expensively framed – but it still came in under the budget that I would have paid for its Austrian equivalent with the excess luggage charge.

I have viewed many masterpieces in Vienna's wonderful museums and art galleries – Klimt's *The Kiss*, Monet's *Waterlilies*, Jacques-Louis David's *Napoleon Crossing the Alps* (you'll know it if you google it). Beauty is most certainly in the eye of the beholder and it is Kasimir's *Melk Abbey* that sits in pride of place above my mantelpiece in my Herefordshire home.

As a postscript to this tale, on 1st January 2018, the New Year's Day concert from Vienna featured a full 30 seconds of drone video footage of Melk Abbey – just long enough for me, squealing with delight, to take a photograph that included both the TV screen and the mantlepiece picture and post it on Facebook with the message:

'Don't you just love it when the picture on the TV is the same building as the etching above the fireplace! The beautiful Melk Abbey as seen on the New Year's Day concert from Vienna. 🎉 Prosit Neujahr to friends and family!'

The final 49 hours

Chapter 17

Never mind

As August 2011 segued into September and the summer activities gave way to the autumn rhythm of commuting to work, I still held on to the excitement of my big day and the mounting challenge of completing Project 4.9.

There is a saying that you can divide people into two groups – those who divide people into two groups and those who don't.

You can also divide people up according to their ability to cope well with last-minute pressure. Some thrive on getting the extra adrenalin buzz that comes with the excitement of the fast-approaching deadline. Others planfully, carefully and thoughtfully avoid last-minute pressure at all costs. It often makes them feel physically sick.

For 49 years, I had skilfully navigated my life's activities with as little last-minute pressure as is humanly possible.

I'd be the person who would arrive so early for their train that they would be able to catch the one before. If I had to go somewhere for a meeting that I had not been to before, I'd often go on a trial run just to work out how long it would take to get there. And then still arrive really early for the meeting.

But 167 days after the start of Project 4.9 (D-day minus two), I had 18 tasks to be completed. 18 left to do in two days! How did that happen to someone who prided themselves on being planful?!

As I woke on day 167, there was a passing thought that maybe, just maybe, I wouldn't complete the project in time. And, anyway, what would it matter? Who would know? Who would care?

And then I got a phone call from a special friend. He was thinking about me and, knowing it was my birthday in two days, rang up to find out how my Project 4.9 was progressing.

I explained that I still had 18 tasks to complete – and he replied with a phrase that was as memorable as it was red rag to a bull: 'Never mind'.

It seemed to unlock a seldom-seen force of nature in me. I am a little unsure of what 'niceties' actually came out of my mouth back to him but, in the remaining few minutes of the call, what I do remember was an alternative script that was running through my mind: 'Never mind! NEVER MIND! Do you realise that you are talking to an international athlete?

There is no way I am not going to achieve this project in time! All I was sharing with you was that I still had 18 tasks to do. Not that I couldn't do them. Never mind! Well, f**k you!'

Having lived a relatively 'planful' life to date, 'Never mind' unlocked an alter ego that I thoroughly enjoyed meeting. The next 48 hours were probably the most eclectic and energising of my life.

Chapter 18

Watch a film

As a young child, there were times (not often) when I succumbed to the wisdom of my parents and watched a TV film that they had recommended.

Those were the days when there were only three TV channels in the UK, when you had to get up and physically change the channel for another programme, and for much of the day there was a test card with a girl, a blackboard and a really creepy clown doll on the TV screen. At night, when the last programme had been transmitted, they actually bid you 'Goodnight' and then played the national anthem before the screen disappeared into a tiny dot.

On one autumn weekend, when the weather must have prevented me from playing outside with my siblings and friends, on my parents' recommendation I sat and watched a captivating black-and-white film starring the then hugely popular actor Kenneth More.

I was at that lovely innocent age when grasping the difference between fact and fiction was still slightly more difficult than it is today (even with 'fake news'), so I was somewhat confused about how the main character, James Hanratty (played by More), could run athletically across fields and down steps, when only the week before I had seen the same man (said Kenneth More) answering to the name Douglas Bader and striding out along a runway on two false legs in the film *Reach for the Sky*.

The film (the one where he runs around a lot) gripped me. It was nostalgic, set in the 1940s, well-acted, scenic, filmed in Scotland and London and, all-in-all, a jolly good whodunnit.

Since that autumnal weekend in my childhood, there have been many remakes of the 'Kenneth More runs around a lot and answers to the name of Hanratty' film and even a stage play. All of which had escaped my attention.

And so, in 2011, as I sat in the Marisco Tavern, fuelled by red wine and fine food, nostalgically reflecting on memories of my childhood and trying to think of tasks that involved the number 49, I was moved by a sudden desire to add to my project list:

Watch The 49 Steps

Accomplishing this particular task presented two fundamental challenges.

- There is not, and in fact to my knowledge never has been, a film called 'The 49 Steps'. The film that I had been so gripped by as an innocent child on a wet autumn afternoon in the late 1960s was Alfred Hitchcock's *The 39 Steps*.

- I only realised this error in my long-term memory two days before my 50th birthday.

Faced with my challenge, I was aware that I had a number of potential options:

1. Ignore the task and fail Project 4.9 (not an option).

2. Admit that I had got the film title wrong and watch *The 39 Steps*.

3. Watch the whole of *The 39 Steps* once and then another circa 24% again (which would be 39 steps plus the equivalent of 10 more steps = 49 steps).

4. Do something else.

Something about the process involved in Option 3 drew my attention to the objects in the film title – namely, 'steps'.

And so, camera in hand, I walked around the house and garden and photographed any and every step I could see, which consisted of: the main staircase (14); garden steps (13); steps into various sheds and rooms (12). Finding myself 10 steps short of the desired target, I was again faced with the prospect of failing this task. Maybe inspired by the lesson learned from the bird task ('Don't forget to look up'), concealed in the landing ceiling was the last of the steps to be photographed – the loft ladder (coming in nicely at 10).

I now had my '49 steps' and all I had to do now was to 'watch' them.

Borrowing the skills learned from being a trained facilitator, in the space of a few minutes, the 12 photographs had been downloaded onto my computer, uploaded into a PowerPoint presentation, configured into a screen show and suitably 'watched'.

Watch The 49 Steps. Tick.

Chapter 19

Postcards

In the flurry of the adrenaline rush of the last few hours, there was one task that I thought might be my downfall; not that it was technically difficult, it was just incredibly labour intensive.

Send 49 postcards

When my grandmother passed away, my brother found in her belongings and returned to me all the postcards I had sent to her over the years. It was like being transported back in time. My very own time machine.

The majority of the earlier postcards were different views of the same location – Tresaith beach, west Wales, our summer holiday location for most of our childhood years.

The message on the back of each postcard comprised pretty much the same sentence stems, with slight variations to the ending on the different cards:

'Thank you for the pocket money, I have spent it on…'

'The journey was…'

'The weather is…'

'See you soon.'

As the years passed and I travelled further afield, the views on the postcards to my grandmother changed to Austria, Australia, Canada or Spain, but the messages on the back remained fairly consistent with my earlier script:

'The weather…'

'The journey…'

'I have bought…'

'See you soon.'

With the advent of first the fax machine and then the internet and social media, I was struck by how special my grandmother's collection was, and wondered: if all the postcards I had sent to people in my life were returned to me at the end of my life, what would they say?

The Project 4.9 task 'Send 49 postcards' gave me the delightful opportunity to surprise people with a personal picture and/or message and to imagine how the bygone tradition of postcard sending would be met by the cards' recipients.

Throughout the 169 days of Project 4.9 I 'regularly' sent my friends and family postcards from Lundy, Vienna, Tresaith and Texas, plus the occasional 'I'm sending this to you just for the fun of it'.

When I say 'regularly', it clearly wasn't regularly enough. With only a few hours left and still a multitude of other activities and tasks to complete and people all over the country aligning like planets in the solar system to converge on my birthday weekend celebrations, I still had to send 16 cards.

When entering into a surge of last-minute, unplanned activity, there is something hugely rewarding about not freezing or feeling sick when totally submerged in the pressure. Novel problem-solving solutions are given the space and freedom to emerge. And so, the under-pressure postcard-sending solution I came up with was, in my mind, a credit to creative thinking. I'd find out whether my plan worked shortly after my birthday.

When I strode to the local royal-red post box on the afternoon before my birthday, pushed the 16 cards into the gaping hole and turned to walk back to the house, I felt like I had just navigated my very own vessel past the snow-capped peak of the last protruding iceberg.

Having completed the task, it was immediately erased from my memory as I moved on to the next pressure-prompted deadline.

Chapter 20

The final countdown

The final 49 hours of life as a 49-year-old were invigoratingly all-consuming.

I called in sick to a three-line whip meeting I was supposed to attend at work.

I chipped golf balls off my father's pristine lawn, avoiding taking divots (not something any half-decent golfer would be proud of) and missing the greenhouse glass that had been the recipient of many a wayward ball in my early years, and also, disappointingly, missing the basket at which I was aiming with 48 of the 49 balls. But more important than that – 'Hit 49 golf balls': Tick. Task completed.

I cooked biscuits and cakes that I then had to put in the freezer, as I had no time to eat them (and later found out were truly inedible anyway).

I planted seeds that I had collected.

I made (more) lists.

I wrote to people.

I took pictures.

I shopped.

I meditated.

I ate.

I celebrated with friends and family.

I smiled and I laughed, and I cried.

And, three days after my birthday, when a manila A5 envelope landed on the door mat of Fairlawn, the family home, and I took out the 16 blank white postcards that I had addressed and sent to myself in that pressure-prompted creative moment three days earlier, I acknowledged that I had indeed creatively completed Project 4.9.

Chapter 21

Write a letter

Of all the tasks that I accomplished on my eclectic journey through the list of 49, there was one that emerged from them all to be deeply precious, like a hidden gem.

Its origins were seeded in Australia.

On 16th December 2006, I was sitting in the WACA Cricket Ground in Perth, watching Australian Adam Gilchrist hit the (then) second-fastest century in Test cricket, when I started up a conversation with a gentleman called Bruce Robertson. At the time, I did not know who he was or what he did and was somewhat surprised that, after only a few minutes, he was asking me what my relationship was like with my father. As someone who prides themself on being able to ask questions of others that get them to reflect on their own life story, I was aware that I was on the receiving end of a very skilful coach.

Bruce was in the middle of writing a book about relationships between fathers and their daughters. As a cricket fan, he had interviewed many international players who had daughters, and was continuing his informal research right here in the hospitality suite at the WACA.

What surprised me most about Bruce was his profession.

He was a (now world-renowned) physician and lung specialist. His interest in the relationship between fathers and daughters stemmed from the fact that so many of his terminally ill male patients told him that one of the greatest regrets of their lives was that they didn't have a better relationship with their daughters.

At the time of my meeting with Bruce, I was holidaying in Australia with my oldest friend. I had known her since we were three. Living two houses away in Church Road, her family was a natural extension of my own. Some months earlier, her father had been diagnosed with terminal cancer.

Taking the opportunity to draw on Bruce's experience, I desperately wanted to find some advice that I could pass on to help her cope with the passing of her father, a truly wonderful man.

Of the many words of advice Bruce offered, one stuck in my memory: 'If you have difficulty telling your father how you feel about him, write him a letter. Before it is too late.'

Write 4 letters

On 3rd September 2011, I wrote four letters, one of which was to my father. Two sides of handwritten scrawl, no more than 100 words. It was a simple message.

I shared with him how much I valued what he had given me throughout my life.

How I admired him.

How grateful I was.

And that I loved him.

On 4th September, as the Mayes family got ready to go out to a restaurant for my birthday meal, my father apologised that he didn't feel well enough to come with us. This was the first time he had ever missed a significant family meal and the poignancy of his decision was hard for me to take. As we left him alone in the family house where he had lived for over 50 years, I realised that I had missed the ideal opportunity to give him the letter.

On our return from the restaurant, I thanked him for the birthday meal (for which he had paid), retrieved his letter from my handbag, handed it to him and left the room.

When I returned a few minutes later, many of the family had now joined him and were sitting chatting about the meal. On the table beside him was the folded letter on top of the open envelope.

My father was a man of habits. You could set your watch by the time he took meals and (due to a medical condition) even the time he would visit the bathroom. And so, with a room full of family, when I saw him get up from his chair and pick up the letter, I knew this was not part of his normal daily routine and that he was in fact taking the letter upstairs to put it somewhere for safe keeping.

As he rose from his chair, he looked me in the eye in a way I had never seen him do before and mouthed to me 'thank you'.

My father passed away two and a half years later.

Of all the 49 tasks that I did in the months between March and September 2011, the act of writing the letter to my father and seeing what my words meant to him was the one that I cherish most.

As I look back now, for me it was the sole (and also the soul) reason for doing Project 4.9.

Postscript

Project 4.9 and the tasks I selected gave me the opportunity to expand my awareness of culture and nature; to do things I'd never done before, or things that I hadn't done in years; to be (relatively) spontaneous; and to celebrate and acknowledge the people and relationships that were most important to me in my life.

I hope that this book has inspired you in some small way to mark the passing of your own years in a creative and imaginative way. I hope also that it may have moved you to connect and reconnect with the people who matter most to you.

The full (and completed) task list

The chapters in which they appear. And a brief comment on those not included in this book.

Chapter	Task
5	List 49 reasons to do this
7	Do 4 gymnastic moves
8	Write a list of the 49 most significant people to me
9	Drive 49 miles
10	Spot and correctly identify 49 different species of birds
11	Make a collage of my 9 favourite books
12	Select from any menu dish number 49
14	Swim 49 strokes with no clothes on
14	Cycle 49 miles
15	Take a 49 bus
16	Buy a painting worth more than £94
18	Watch 49 Steps
19	Send 49 postcards
20	Hit 49 golf balls
21	Write 4 letters

Task	Do the lottery using numbers 1 4 9
Response	I won £10 on my first lottery ticket, but because the point of the activity was to learn how to do the lottery and didn't extend to 'how to claim a prize', I never got round to getting the money!
Task	Write a list of 49 things to do before I die
Response	Also known as my 'bucket list'. I have been working my way though it ever since.
Task	Kiss 4 men
Response	I couldn't possibly comment.
Task	Write a list of 49 places to see before I die
Response	The list exists; visiting them is proving to be more challenging. Here's hoping I live long enough to see the end of 'pandemic-disrupted' global travel.
Task	Try 9 new places to eat
Response	For a food-lover, this task was very satisfying.
Task	Celebrate my birthday with 49 people
Response	The night before my birthday, a group of friends from school, all of whom were 50 in the same school year, met for a barge trip up (and back down) the Severn. The following day, I celebrated with my close family. The day after, I was with a group of colleagues, who raised a glass to celebrate my landmark birthday. When I counted the number of people involved over the three-day period, the number came, spookily, to exactly 49.

Task	**Read 4 new authors**
Response	Kathryn Stockett (*The Help*); Rachel Simon (*The Story of Beautiful Girl*); Kate Atkinson (*Started Early, Took My Dog*); Tatiana de Rosnay (*Sarah's Key*).
Task	**Learn 49 new German words**
Response	The combination of being awful at languages and the bombardment of stimuli in the 169 days of Project 4.9 meant I did indeed learn 49 new German words, but now have no recollection of which ones they were.
Task	**Buy 49 new things**
Response	Really easy to do if you avoid second-hand shops.
Task	**List 4 men I'd like to have slept with**
Response	███████████████████████ The names have been redacted to protect the identities of the innocent, and quite possibly oblivious, 4 men.
Task	**List 49 favourite songs**
Response	Yep, another list…
Task	**Cook 4 new things**
Response	Dreadful sugar-free biscuits (inedible); equally dreadful sugar-laden brownies (also inedible); apfelstrudel (nothing like my mother's or my cousin Lotte's); and rice pudding (much, much better than the tinned stuff). And, yes, I do have a sweet tooth.

Task	Walk 49 miles
Response	I'd like to report that I did the walk all in one go, raising thousands of pounds for charity. I didn't. I covered the distance over seven days (recorded by my pedometer) during my stay in Vienna (and on the days when I wasn't cycling to nudist beaches).
Task	Do 4 childhood things
Response	Played on the swings; jumped in a puddle; skipped in the street; wee'd on the back lawn (not all on the same day, and none of them in view of anyone else).
Task	Have coffee with 9 people I haven't seen in 9 months
Response	I spent a lot of time in high-street coffee shops in 2011.
Task	Write a 49-word poem
Response	I remember where I wrote it (Vienna), why I wrote it (a £1 million project was about to crash), what mood I was in (desperate) and the effect of writing it (calming). Sadly, however, I have no recollection of the 49 words I wrote.
Task	Take 49 pictures and save them
Response	The pictures I took are a lovely keepsake to remind me of my final 169-days of my forties. I keep them in a folder saved on my computer desktop.

Task	Plant 4 things
Response	Having been given the birth name of Rosemary, I felt it was fitting to grow 4 herbs (from seeds in little pots) – dill, thyme, parsley and basil.
Task	Swim 49 lengths
Response	On a work trip to the States, I stayed in a hotel with a spa pool that was so small that you could almost touch both sides. It was the perfect size for someone lacking aquatic endurance fitness to complete this task.
Task	Visit 49 new websites
Response	This was in the days before Facebook would take me on a similar journey, unconsciously, and in a fraction of the time.
Task	Meditate for 49 minutes
Response	A peaceful pause in an emotionally turbulent time.
Task	Buy 49 things with 49 on
Response	In my imagination I thought I would be buying lots of brightly coloured t-shirts and San Francisco 49s kit but, as time ran out and desperation kicked in, items that qualified for this task included Austrian stationery that cost 4.90 Euros (and had a price sticker on the item) and 15 last-minute lottery tickets (bought just so that I could complete the task), none of which won anything.
Task	List 4 favourite films (that aren't in my book-cover collage)
Response	*The Sting, The Third Man, The Horse Whisperer, The Thomas Crown Affair.*

Task	Have a celebratory drink on 17th July (49 days before my birthday)
Response	It involved one of the four men I kissed, so I couldn't possibly comment.
Task	Go round 9 holes in 49 shots (golf)
Response	This took place on a putting green – much quicker and much easier to count the shots.
Task	Eat 49 different fruits
Response	I didn't realise how difficult it would be to find 49 different fruits when you shop in traditional UK supermarkets. In desperation, a subtle rule change was invoked, which meant that fresh mango and dried mango counted as two different fruits. (The 49th and final piece of fruit (dried mango) was eaten at 6pm on 3rd September 2011.)
Task	Pamper yourself in 4 ways
Response	Fish pedicure (anyone else remember these?!); conventional pedicure (no animals/fish involved); back massage; Indian head massage.
Task	List 49 best jobs in the world
Response	Yep, yet another 49-item list.
Task	Buy 4 items of clothing I've never bought before
Response	What better excuse for me to try out a personal styling experience in a London department store? (You know, the experience where a shop assistant chooses items for you that you would never think of choosing. You buy them at great expense. And then wear them only once.)

Task	List 9 things I'd do with £49,000
Response	Another one of my lists, but at least this list was only 9 items long.
Task	List 9 iconic images
Response	Another one of my 'at least this list was only 9 items long' lists.
Task	49 new LinkedIn connections
Response	Ah, what a novelty LinkedIn was back in 2011.
Task	Juggle 4 balls 49 times
Response	After weeks and weeks of practice, and rising performance anxiety that was proportionate to the fast-approaching deadline date of 4.9.11, this was achieved, only once, and with a disproportionate sense of relief, on the back lawn of the family home, on 2nd September 2011 (just before my trip to the Golden City for menu number 49).
Task	Buy 49 varieties of Heinz
Response	The look from the check-out person at the supermarket was delightful to observe, as she scanned my 49 individual tins.

Memoirs of Childhood and Youth

Another thought moves me when I think back of my youth: that so many people gave me something or were something to me without being aware of it. Some with whom I had never exchanged a word, some even whom I had only heard mentioned have had a definite influence on me. They entered my life and became forces within me. Much that I would not have sensed so clearly or done with such determination otherwise I feel and do because I am as if under the compulsion of those people. Therefore I believe that we all live spiritually of what others gave us in significant moments of our lives. These significant moments do not announce themselves but come unexpectedly. They also do not make a show of themselves but appear inconspicuous. Sometimes they even acquire their significance only in our memory, just as the beauty of a work of music or of a landscape reveals itself only in memory. Much of what has become our own gentleness, kindness, ability to forgive, truthfulness, faithfulness, submission in suffering we owe to people in whom we experienced these qualities, whether in an important or unimportant event. A thought turned life lept into us like a spark and kindled a flame within us. … If those who have become a blessing to us were present with us and if we could tell them how they did, they would be surprised of what flowed from their lives into ours.

Albert Schweitzer, *Memoirs of Childhood and Youth*, translated by Kurt Bergel and Alice R. Bergel (Syracuse: Syracuse University Press, 1997), 81-82. © Syracuse University Press. Reproduced with permission from the publisher.

About the author

Rosie Mayes was born in Gloucestershire, the daughter of an Austrian mother and English father.

She is a qualified teacher, sports scientist and coach and has co-authored literature on Leadership.

She currently lives in Herefordshire and can occasionally be found cycling in Vienna or wandering around Lundy.